I0003056

AS HEARD ON THE INTERNET

A COMMON SENSE

BUSINESS BOOK

Also by the Author

Kill the First Tiger
(A Common Sense Business Book)

The Five Reasons Why
Cricket is More American Than Baseball

AS HEARD ON THE INTERNET

A COMMON SENSE
BUSINESS BOOK

Michael F. Johnson

Print ISBN   978-0-9881748-1-8

eBook ISBN   978-0-9881748-8-7

Editor's Note

I first met Michael Johnson many years ago, in the afternoon of the fourth day of our company's week-long annual sales meeting. We had been treated to so many presentations throughout the week that, just maybe, our eagerness and attentiveness were now wanting. Perhaps it was just me who had started to sense a sameness to each session. I doubt it, though.

More than just the carefully designed PowerPoint template that someone high up in executive class had mandated and that someone low down in marketing had agonized over and disseminated to all presenters (for the sake of branding), the sense of sameness derived from hearing too many times how well positioned we were to move forward, and how we were to incentivize and monetize, to increase market share, to embrace metrics-based decision-making, to engage with our customers by tying ropes around them, to find synergy, to leverage best practices and our core competencies... mostly recited word for word from the endless "decks." Well, you get my point.

Then it was Michael's turn. In these days, he sported a pony tail. So that was different. I handed him the clicker so he could navigate through his deck at his own speed. He brought up his first slide, and put down the clicker. On one slide five bullet points, black on white, clearly expressed what he was working on, where he and his development team were, when they would finish, what he would hand to us, and how we were to take it to market. We were, all, wide awake again. Any questions?

This book reminds me of that day. There is no clutter. All chapters are short and to the point. They were born as podcasts, and here we have collected a year's worth, dressed them up a little for this medium, and now offer them in their brilliant clarity.

It's a small book, a short read, but of large ideas and grand topics. There is nothing hifalutin' here, simply comments and thoughts that self-evidently define common sense. You might blow your way through these chapters in one go, or pick a random starting point, or look for a topic that is especially pertinent to your situation. However you go about it, I expect you'll come back to it.

"As Heard on The Internet" complements and supplements Michael's first book, "Kill the First Tiger." I hope you enjoy these additional Common Sense Comments.

August, 2016

Dedication

In my working life I have had the wonderful blessing of some fantastic mentors, peers, and staff. All of them have made me a better person.

In their own way, they have proven to me that using Common Sense is the only way to effectively run a business.

To Them.

LOOK, MA, I WROTE ANOTHER BUSINESS BOOK!

Table of Contents

AS HEARD ON THE INTERNET

A COMMON SENSE BUSINESS BOOK

PREFACE

I have been working since I was 13 years old, when I started my first media distribution company (I delivered the Washington Star) and my first property maintenance company (I cut lawns, raked leaves, and shoveled snow.) Even in those early days, I learned a tremendous amount about what to do and what not to do to be successful in business.

My next career was in retail. I spent seven years working for William Hahn & Company, one of America's absolute best shoe retailers. I loved the shoe business and the retail business. As a third generation "shoe-dog," I figured I had found my place in life and would just continue to grow my career with Hahn's. Here again, I learned a tremendous amount from all those around me, especially from the more senior men and women in the organization. To this day, I strongly argue that there is no better business educational program than starting as low man in the stock room of a well-run retailer and then working your way up the organizational ladder.

As detailed in my book, *Kill the First Tiger,* my career at Hahn's came to a rapid stop while I was still in my 20s. In a textbook case of lack of common sense, the firm that bought Hahn's failed to understand the business or its customers, and then they destroyed it. It took the new owners less than ten years to completely dismantle a century-old, revered retail chain. In the end, there was nothing left except empty storefronts and broken dreams.

Next up, I went back to school and got a degree in computer programming. In one way or another, I have been involved in the blend between technology and business ever since. The first ten years or so were spent designing, developing, and deploying software and systems. The next ten saw a shift into senior leadership roles, initially in technology only and then running full P&L groups. Common Sense was always with me and always proved the best way to approach opportunities and challenges.

In 2008, at the beginning of the worst U.S. economic collapse since the Great Depression, I founded a strategic consulting firm called Full Potential Associates. We focus on the high-level blend of business, technology, and education.

Full Potential Associates is all about common sense. We take a very direct, open, and honest approach to every client engagement. We turn away more clients than we take on to ensure that, when we do engage, we can provide quality advice to clients who can and will use it.

We prefer to offer free advice—sometimes telling the client to simply not do what they are planning to do— in order to best serve the client, rather than taking an assignment where we cannot provide actionable advice.

Over a year ago, in response to the urging of many of our clients, and with the tremendous support of ValidTangent Media, I started a weekly podcast called *Common Sense Comments* (mfjspeaker.podbean.com). Each week we release a new episode, typically of three minutes or less, and each episode contains a Common Sense Approach to help the listener consider how they could address a similar situation in their business life.

This book is the written transcription of some of those Common Sense Comments episodes, selected from the more than 55 that have been broadcast to date.

I hope you enjoy the book as much as I enjoyed writing and recording the podcast episodes.

Ability

Over the past few weeks I've been spending a lot of time with folks from the human resources community. It seems that most open positions in the business world today require so many abilities that virtually no one person could possess them all. The HR folk even have a phrase for this phenomenon–they call this impossible candidate *A Purple Squirrel.*

As I listen to both the HR folks and to frustrated hiring managers, I hear an impossibly long list of required abilities. I also hear about a legion of applicants who do not have these abilities. To me, it seems like both numbers are too high. It also seems like some creative **ability** would come in handy here.

I spend a lot of my consulting time working in the education marketplace. Believe me, colleges and universities are doing the best they can to produce quality candidates. Despite their efforts, there is a growing mismatch between abilities attained and abilities requested.

This mismatch has created a bizarre employment situation where companies can't grow because they feel they can't find staff with the right abilities, and workers can't find jobs that match the abilities they do have.

As is often said in the sporting world, being available–AVAIL-ABILITY–is the most important ability of all. If a pitcher has a blazing fastball but can't pitch when his turn comes up, what good is he? If a running back has tremendous power and agility but can't stay on the field because he is out of shape, what good is he? If a soccer goalie just can't be scored on but she can't play because of discipline issues, what good is she? Without AVAILABILITY, no other abilities matter.

A prospective employee, being right there in front of you, ready and willing to learn new skills and help a company grow, should count for something. Balance that against that seemingly perfect fit person who isn't available (or may not even exist).

Which one will bring more value to the current project? The one who could start on Monday, doing something and learning as they go, or the one who you may never get? The available one sounds good to me.

Which one will push themselves harder? The one seeking to add more abilities or the one who already has what you think you want?

The Common Sense Approach here is to understand and accept that the eager, hard-working, **available** people tend to make great hires and can make a quick and powerful impact within your company. As I said earlier, the best ability might just be **AVAIL-ability.**

Ads

Let's talk about one of everybody's favorite topics: advertisements. Okay, maybe ads are not one of everybody's favorites, but certainly they are a key element of any capitalist society.

Firms spent about $600 billion on ads worldwide in 2015, with about 30% of that being directed at the U.S. market alone. Even in a very tough global economy, ad spending was up over six percent. All indications are that 2016 will be another huge year in spending with another nice increase.

Okay, so, ads. Big deal. We all know all about ads.

Well, here's the thing; Interpublic, which is a massive ad agency, predicts that online ads may surpass TV ads in 2017. That is next year, people.

So, I ask you, what is your company doing about this shift? Some very large firms that failed to embrace upcoming and incoming waves of technology change have suffered mightily.

Borders' (the former bookstore chain) un-willingness to participate in web-commerce in a meaningful way led to its corporate suicide. Microsoft, who missed and then badly misplayed the cell phone/smart phone wave, has written off billions of dollars as a result.

A great deal of my strategy consulting work is focused on helping firms understand, and then adapt to, the never-ending forward march of technology. My clients look to me as both a readying and a steadying force with regard

7

to how technology will impact their business and the markets they serve.

As this transition from TV ads to online continues to happen, I have a question for you: Is your business ready? Even if your business is in a market that doesn't do a lot of advertising, the shift will still impact you on at least two fronts.

First, your competitors may use this shift to start advertising. Then you may become the odd man out by not being there. Second, you customers *will* be seeing these ads online, for your products or not, and they will come to expect you to interact with them in that manner.

This is another huge shift in customer interaction. Through the years these shifts have presented both problems and opportunities for businesses, regardless of the markets they serve. Things like toll-free numbers, fax machines, websites, e-Commerce, and apps have all dramatically impacted the way companies interact with their customers.

So, ask again: Is your company ready?

The Common Sense Approach here is to wake up and see what is happening all around you. Get online, get mobile, and get to it now.

Arc

A great deal of business management literature today tells us to shoot for the moon, have big, audacious goals, or other superlative-laden concepts.

While aspiring to greatness is a wonderful way to drive your work, it is not a *task* on which you can actually work. In simple terms, just wanting to *have* great results does not *create* great results.

Too many business leaders today are focused on the end of the process, without understanding the starting line and the real work that is required to get to that end.

In my consulting practice I do a significant amount of strategy work. Oftentimes, I get the call after a few failed attempts to realize a strategy. In these situations, I often deliver a talk of mine called *The Arc of the Corporate*. It isn't the word of God, but it is the truth. Since that talk typically runs 60 to 90 minutes, I'll give you just a taste of it now.

Picture an arc flowing from the lower left up into the upper right. *The Arc of the Corporate* begins at the top right with the *Desirable*, then moves downward to the left to the *Probable*, and finally rests at the lower left on the *Doable*.

While everybody wants to focus their energy on the ideal outcome—the *Desirable*—they rarely understand all the hard work necessary to reach that outcome. Therefore, you simply can't start here.

Even when the arc is moved downward to the *Probable* stage, the gap between *Probable* and current is too great for it to serve as a starting point.

It is only when we move the arc down to the *Doable* stage that can we build realistic and executable plans of action. If you start anywhere along the arc other than the *Doable* stage, you simply will not advance any further **up** the arc. In fact, you will slide down, if not off, the arc entirely.

You must keep the *Desirable* in mind as an end goal, and the *Probable* in mind as a stop along the way. However, you must start doing at the *Doable*.

The Common Sense Approach here is to understand that no matter how lofty the end goal, you cannot start at the end. Aim for it, yes. Begin with it, no. Follow the arc properly and you will reach your desired goal.

Babies

A very dear friend of mine has a relatively new grandson. Thankfully, the child is happy, healthy, and truly a cute little guy. This is not the case with all the babies I see. The hard truth is some babies are ugly. Sorry to say it, but I must speak the truth.

In the case of my friend, we are spared the very uncomfortable conversations where one tries to find kind things to say about the baby without addressing the fact that it is not beautiful.

To some business people, their products, their office buildings, their new advertising campaigns are their babies. Think about it. How many times have you heard things like, "Our new TV ads are Billy's baby," or, "From buying the land, to the first shovel of dirt, all the way to the ribbon cutting, this building has been Sally's baby."?

Herein lies the dilemma. Not all babies are adorable. Some products don't fit a market need. Some ad campaigns don't resonate with customers. Regardless of how often people ask you to be honest, nobody wants to hear that their baby isn't beautiful.

Now, ugly babies often grow to be good-looking youngsters, and some even end up being beautiful women and handsome men. Even if their looks don't change, those babies can grow up to cure cancer, write wonderful books, or make other important contributions to society.

The same can be true for those products, office buildings, and ad campaigns. A new version of that initially weak software platform may be just what the market needed. A green roof plan on that unattractive building can

11

dramatically cut energy costs and provide a great outdoor meeting space. The TV ad that bombed at first can become a YouTube sensation, bringing a whole new customer base to your firm.

Many of my clients open an engagement by doing the business equivalent of showing me pictures of their babies; product demos, strategic plans, market studies, and the like. My first course of action is to help them see those pictures for what they actually show rather than through the misty eyes of a proud parent or a doting grandparent.

Everything, including babies, doesn't have to be beautiful to be wonderful. However, you do need to **truly see** each aspect of your business so that you can take whatever action is appropriate case by case.

The Common Sense Approach here is to look at all your business babies with clear eyes and then do whatever is needed to help them grow up and contribute to your family of products. Now, that would make a beautiful picture.

Bacon

I love bacon. I really, really love bacon. To me, it is the perfect food. It goes with everything and it's also awesome all by itself.

Let's say you run a business that makes bacon. And let's say you make the best bacon ever. Great deal, right? You make a product loved by everyone. It is a perfect situation. You love bacon, I love bacon, your bacon is great. All is well.

You continue to make great bacon. Business will continue to grow probably forever. You will conquer the world with bacon.

Well, hmmm... maybe not. Tragically, even bacon has a downside. You see, not everybody loves bacon. I realize that this is hard to imagine. However, it is true.

For starters, there are over 2.1 billion people in the world who *can't* eat bacon due to religious, health, or societal issues. That's almost 30% of the population. Think about that for a minute: almost 30% of the world's population *can't* eat bacon. Add to that group the people who just *don't* eat bacon and you now have a significant portion of the population of "non-customers" for your bacon business.

I do a fair amount of public speaking. Many of my speeches contain ideas about how to position your business to reach its full potential. Part of that positioning is understanding how big your business could become by gaining insight into the total available market. From there, you can build actionable strategies to capture that market.

As I mentioned earlier, you can't sell bacon to everybody in the world no matter how good your bacon is. If you just keep doing what you are doing, making great bacon, you will *never* reach that 30+% of the population who don't eat bacon.

Once you understand and accept that, you can make informed choices. You can decide to reshape your expectations of selling bacon to everyone. You can make bacon out of things other than pigs, or any kind of meat. You can expand your business to sell things that aren't bacon.

Any of those choices, and no doubt some others, could be viable alternatives to help ensure the continued growth of your business.

The Common Sense Approach here is to understand that no matter how good your product is, there will absolutely be people, perhaps large groups of them, who won't buy it. Understand that and then make whatever adjustments you feel necessary to keep you cooking.

Barbers

No matter what websites or news sources you use, it is impossible to miss out on reports about the problems businesses are having finding enough quality talent. It would seem all the world's business problems could be solved if companies could just hire more people.

Over the years I've worked for and consulted with companies large and small all around the world. To be honest, I can't think of a single circumstance where **not having enough employees** was actually the core problem facing a business.

My experience has taught me that business leaders today suffer **far more** from a lack vision and focus rather than from a shortage of talented people to hire.

Very few business problems require a large number of people to solve them. In fact, I would say the opposite is true. A small, tightly focused and self-directed group of people can get an awful lot more done than a large group of committee- and meeting-laden people.

All of this reminds me of an old country expression:

Hiring a dozen barbers won't get you a faster haircut.

In my consulting practice, it is not unusual for me to be asked to help firms generate quality ideas more quickly, bring products to market more quickly, or both. Very rarely is the solution to bring on more people. Almost always, the issue is one of focusing the existing resources rather than the need for more people.

Throwing people at the problem almost never helps and typically makes the problem worse.

Without a clear vision, and the associated support, companies tend to add people to address *this* tangential issue or *that* non-core piece of business.

Before you know it, you've got dozens of barbers and you are still not giving faster haircuts. Along the way, the things that should command your company's undivided attention are only partially addressed and grow worse by the day.

Sadly, this often leads to even more people being hired, as this is an easier process than having leadership slow down and then clarify and communicate what is truly important.

The Common Sense Approach here is to develop and share a clear vision for the company. Align your people to that vision and let them go and realize it. Once you do those things, your company should look razor sharp.

Be Tall School

Ladies and gentlemen, I am here to announce the next great development in business: Be Tall School. That's right, you too can be tall if you just come to my new school. If you are already tall, my school can make you taller! Just attend these classes and we can show you how to be tall! Once you know how it is done, you can just do it.

Ok, so I was kidding about that *be tall* thing. However, I did it with serious intent, to address another idea–almost as ridiculous– which has actually taken root in American business: the idea that Leadership can be taught.

There seems to be an endless stream of leadership books, seminars, and classes available from another endless stream of leadership gurus. Each of these leadership experts presents their leadership lessons as though they are the *true* and *final* word on the topic.

Just send your money, buy the book, attend the classes, or watch the webcast, and we can **teach** you how to be a leader. We are successful CEOs, military officials, sporting superstars, business school deans, and political leaders. We have done leadership the right way and we can teach you how to do it, too!

Well, my lifetime of business experience tells me something very different. You see, I don't believe that leadership can be taught at all. It can be learned, certainly, but not taught. Leadership is a nuanced art, not a scientific principle. All too frequently people today confuse leadership with management. Worse yet, they use the words interchangeably.

In the real world, leadership is the way a person feels, thinks, and interacts with others. It is not about measuring monthly targets, seeking to increase sales by X%, or making sure manufacturing cost ratios are in check. Those are all important tasks, and leaders do them, but that is not leadership.

Leaders are born to it. Sometimes it's obvious early in life. These are the girls whom other students naturally follow due to that certain presence or vision. These are the boys whom others rally behind to support a cause and drive for change.

Sometimes it takes a bit longer for leadership to develop. These are the men and women who later in life get chosen or elected to positons of responsibility (be it foreman of the jury, project team lead, or mayor) because others believe in them and are willing to follow their lead. They earn and get promotions once they come into their natural leadership.

Leadership is within certain people, be it shown at an early age, in their teens or 20s, or perhaps into their second or third careers. More often than not, the leadership trait doesn't surface for one reason or another. A portion of my consulting work is to help identify the actual leaders within my clients' firms. A larger portion of my work is helping to identify those who are leaders in title only.

It is certainly true that some leaders need courses, mentors, and life experiences (good or ill) to bring out the leader in them. It is equally, and more importantly, true that you can't teach just anybody to be a leader.

It is a significant waste of resources to try and turn people into leaders. It is folly to believe that even your best workers would, should, or could just be taught how to be leaders. You might as well send them to Be Tall School.

An example I cite regularly is computer programming. I'm confident I can teach any one of you to program computers. However, that will not make you a programmer. Being a programmer requires a certain type of mind, mindset, and personality. You either are one or you are not.

There are all types of leaders and all types of leadership styles. Some lead from behind, some by example, some with an open door, and some with an iron fist. Each is effective in their own way.

The Common Sense Approach here is to be a leader yourself and to find the natural leaders within your organization. Then do whatever is necessary to bring out that natural talent to let the leader inside emerge.

Beach House

Many companies consider buying other companies a key growth strategy. Of course, there is nothing wrong with that, provided the buying goes well.

Acquisitions is a tricky business. There are so many factors to consider before the transaction actually happens. How to value the target firm? How will the marketplace view this purchase? Who will get which job in the new firm?

Then there are the real practical problems that happen once the deal is done. Closing down the Colesville office was costlier than originally planned. More customers than projected leave the new firm. A lawsuit pops up over a severance package.

I've participated in many acquisitions, several from each side of table. My experiences have taught me that the key factor that determines if a purchase pays off in the long run is the patience of the acquirer. It is rarely the deal itself or the firm acquired that causes the problem. It is the unwillingness to exercise the patience and discipline required to see the plan through.

I liken buying another business to the idea of adding a beach house rental to your overall property portfolio. If you find the right place, pay a fair price, and take good care of it, the rental should contribute solid and regular profits for a long time. All good, right?

Sadly, many acquiring firms do not extend the required patience to have these deals truly pan out. Picture this: another house starts renting cheaper, and Finance deviates from the plan and decides to cut back on expenses by turning off the A/C. Then your new property misses an

20

annual sales target and the CEO decides to cancel the boat slip lease.

That great property you bought has years of great promise. Now, with intermittent A/C and no boat slip, it is suddenly un-rentable. A great addition to the portfolio has now become a tragic loss to the company as people don't want beach houses with no A/C and no boat slip.

The Common Sense Approach here is to build a good acquisition plan and stick to it long enough to see if it really works. You bought that beach house for a reason, and you must stay focused on what the reason was. You can then enjoy the waterfront sunrises each and every morning for years to come.

Beer Me

In this chapter I'd like to discuss two things I'm passionate about: business and beer. You would have to look incredibly hard to find a tougher business market than beer. Yet, new and innovative beers continue to be brewed and the brewers who make them continue to be successful.

Beer has been around pretty much since the dawn of agriculture. Talk about a legacy business! Yet, innovation continues. Beer is one of the most heavily regulated, controlled, and taxed products in the world. Beer was even illegal in the U.S. during Prohibition. Talk about a difficult legislative environment! Yet, an average of 1.5 new breweries *a day* opened in the U.S. during 2014.

Beyond just being tasty, beer offers us plenty of business lessons. As mentioned earlier, beer has been a business almost forever **and** beer exists under very hostile business conditions. Even under these settings, breweries continue to innovate and to grow.

While the business of beer provides us with much to discuss, I think the most interesting aspect is how breweries continue to grow their business. Compare and contrast these two paths. At one extreme we have the mega merger—AB-InBev and SABMiller are in the process of combining their operations in a $100+ billion transaction. This is a classic business play of buying your way into growth and market dominance. The combined firm will have a world-wide presence and will be a market leader in many different countries.

At the other extreme we have Wisconsin's own New Glarus Brewing Company. New Glarus absolutely refuses to sell its beer outside of the state of Wisconsin.

Yes, New Glarus has chosen to limit its distribution to a state that has just over five million residents. There is almost daily pressure, especially from customers in the neighboring states, to expand. New Glarus is steadfast in their decision. New Glarus brews amazing beer and also gets amazing business results. Even with their self-imposed market limits, they are among the top 20 independent breweries in the country.

My consulting work takes me from back-of-napkin startups all the way up to multi-billion dollar, multi-national firms. Like the beer examples discussed here, I've seen many ways to grow a business and I've helped many companies with that growth.

Which kind of business do you want to be? A sprawling multinational or a tight local firm? There isn't a right or wrong answer to how to grow your business. The key thing stopping you from growing your business is your dedication to **how** you want your business to grow.

The Common Sense Approach here is to dig deep and determine what you want your business to be. Once you decide, keep your focus **on** and stay committed **to** whatever is needed to keep you on that business growth path. With hard thinking and the associated hard work, who knows what's on tap for your future?

Bit by Bit

Money has always been a bit of a funny thing. Even when coins had value due to the metal used to mint them, there was always a bit of a game that everybody played; I give you this shiny thing and you give me a flagon of ale.

Paper money never made any sense at all since it had no immediate value as an object. From the very first notes or drafts, it was always about a promise that you could take this paper someplace else and get something of value. When paper currency was "backed" by the gold or silver standard, that promise at least had a chance to be true.

Currencies are no longer backed. Now we just accept that the issuing government will honor the promise. They back the promise to get everybody in on the game. I give you this papery sort of thing and you give me a meal, a piece of furniture, or a few gallons of gas.

We are all in on the game even if none of us knows what the rules are or how any of us can win. As long as we all believe that some government still guarantees the promise, we can all just keep playing.

Things like credit cards, debit cards, and PayPal have made paying for things almost frictionless. More recent developments like Google Wallet and Apple Pay have made paying even easier. These technologies have also put us at a greater distance from physical money. Add in peer-to-peer payments like Venmo and people can pay each other without touching money.

In the last few years, a different type of technology has begun to separate the money promise from any national government. I'm talking about Bitcoin and the various other non-governmental crypto-currencies. Beyond the great technology being used, a key appeal factor is that these digital currencies aren't controlled by any government. The promise of value remains, but rather than by a country the promise is kept by a wide and diverse group of technology geniuses.

This is no fringe movement. Very serious financial firms are providing funding for these efforts. Very serious tech firms, IBM among them, are working on the coding. Nationless money is already happening now, and acceptance grows daily.

Imagine the policy, process, and accounting changes that are impacted by an all-digital and nationless currency. The near future could hold no cash registers, no change given back, and no foreign exchange fees.

The Common Sense Approach here is to understand how even something as fundamental as physical money is being disrupted by technology. Understand how this impacts your customers and your business and then make the necessary adjustments. Maybe you can learn a bit and then you can cash in on all these changes.

Business Diet

Let's talk about the business diet. No, this isn't some new culinary craze to compete with something you saw on TV or in a magazine. It is about health, for sure, but not about your body. This is about the health of your business.

Diet isn't automatically a bad thing. Diet just means what one consumes, not how much. Eating pizza three times a day, every day, is still a diet. However, I just doubt it would lead to any slimming of the waistline. Or you could eat only amazingly healthy foods but in portions that are super-sized and still not do your waistline any good. Like most things in life, your diet should be balanced in order to obtain consistently good outcomes.

So if diet is what we consume, and keeping in mind this is about your business, not your body, what are you giving your company to eat? Every fork full of debt, outdated machinery, and short-sighted financial actions takes you one step closer to the E.R. Likewise, every balanced meal of innovation, long-term strategy, and responsive employment policies helps keep the company young and strong.

Are you feeding your company a steady diet of whatever it has been eating for the past ten or 20 years? The same type of products, processes, and personnel? If your company is healthy and living well, that might not be a bad thing. But even if your company is healthy, you still need to mind the diet. Your company, like your body, is constantly aging, and you need to consider what changes would be good for your company diet as the aging process continues. Are you trying new things like process improvement, agile development, overseas partners, and a strong technology plan?

Perhaps your college-age diet is no longer appropriate for where your company is now. If your company is not as healthy as you would like, what dietary changes are you reviewing? Is there too much fat in your headcount? Would some leaner inventory processes help get things back on track? Do you need to eat some of that strange social media or mobile technology stuff? Keep in mind that making the changes now, while you are still in OK health, is far less painful and far less expensive than the surgery required to address a chronic problem.

If you let your health slip far enough, something more urgent and radical may be necessary to stop your company from dying. You make have to seek immediate treatment and make moves like closing a plant, selling off a division, or surgically removing a large group of staff.

As you run your business day to day, think about what you are feeding it day to day. Consider each meeting, quarterly review, maintenance contract, and other automatic "meals" as the diet of your business. Take into account if this next trip, that standing company policy, or even the old headquarters building is something you want to feed your business.

As you are planning for your business over the longer term, think about the current health of your company, the diet you are feeding it, and how you will measure your company's health at the end of the planning period.

In my strategy work with clients, we always consider the impact of each mouthful of the company diet and the effect it has on the company's overall health, both short and long term. There is no harm in having the bacon in your diet that may be represented as a generous employee leave policy. There is also no point in having the tofu of cost reduction in your diet if it only represents a short-term mindset that creates a strong quarter but not long-lasting business health.

The Common Sense Approach here is to realize that your company's long-term health is determined by what you feed it. Just like with a human body, you get fat or get healthy one fork full at time. Just remember, it is OK to leave room for some bacon.

Company

Simply put, a company is a collection of people brought together to serve a single purpose that could not be done well, if at all, by one person.

For a business, that single purpose is the efficient creation and distribution of products and services for which the business could charge enough to make a profit.

In the U.S. we have many types of business companies: LLCs, 'S' Corporations, and 'C' Corporations, to name a few.

Beyond the business world, there are many other types of companies. From the creative community, we have opera companies, theater companies, and dance companies.

We also have firefighter companies. In fact, even the U.S. Army groups soldiers into companies. Who can forget the "Boogie Woogie Bugle Boy of Company B"?

Whether they are formed to build products, sing arias, dance The Nutcracker, put out fires, or protect the country, the core reason **every company** is created remains the same: people working together to accomplish more than one person could do alone.

So the question is; Does your company behave with that in mind?

In my consulting practice, I am often asked to address what appears to be a complex operational or technical problem. Once I get into deeper conversations with the key staff, I typically find that the company is not acting collaboratively and with a single purpose. Rather, they are acting like a series of smaller groups with each one doing what they think is best.

Organizations tend to drift off target when leadership loses focus on that singular goal. Well-meaning people, with good minds and good intentions, dilute the company's resources and actually prevent the company's success because of the lack of focus.

Changing directions, adding new products, opening new offices, entering new markets are all fine and they could bring great benefit to your company. However, you need to make sure your entire staff **understands** why the company is doing these new things. That way, they can unite around this new singular purpose.

As long as everybody knows why they are doing what they are asked to do and why the **company** has chosen this current path, they can remain unified, and therefore more effective, in all of their efforts.

The Common Sense Approach here is to remember why your company was formed in the first place. Review everything your company is doing now and make whatever adjustments are necessary to get the whole organization working toward the same unified goal. Once you have done that, you will be in the **company** of America's best firms.

Culture Club

Today's business news is full of stories stressing the importance of changing your corporate culture.

The general idea seems to be that your company needs a new culture—one that proposes this new theory or that new trend, one that ensures you are up to date and "with it."

The culture of a business is the natural expression and extension of the leadership of that business. If the culture of the founder, the CEO, the family, or whoever runs the business no longer suits the needs of the business, then the focus should be on the leadership, not the employees.

A quick Amazon book search for "change corporate culture" returns over 4,300 hits. A Google search for "corporate culture articles" yields almost 20 million hits.

It would seem that there are a lot of authors, consultants, and business speakers out there who will tell you what is wrong with your business culture and what you **must do** to change it. They all want to hit you with the Culture Club, change how your business operates, and "fix" you.

Of course, as an author, consultant, and a speaker I don't want to talk ill of my brethren. However, on this specific topic I must stray from popular opinion. In fact, I would like to swing the Culture Club at **them** in defense of what **you** have done to bring your business to where it is today.

Since the leaders set, pattern, and reinforce their culture throughout the business, if any culture change is required it must come from the top.

My consulting work brings me into contact with firms that are facing the disconnect between the way they have always done things and the way things need to be done today.

Sometimes, a family business isn't transitioning well to the next generation. Sometimes, it is the Founder's Dilemma, where the business has simply outgrown the expertise of the people who started it. Regardless of the cause, your company may still need a culture change.

But before you go about trying to change your company culture, I suggest you take a look at how closely your company reflects you as a person. Has the company become disconnected from what you intended? Do the employees act as you would and thereby accurately reflect your culture?

It is very possible that the only change you need is a return to the original culture and to reconnect your employees to it, rather than shifting to a new one.

The Common Sense Approach here is to reflect on what made your company special in the first place. If that original culture still works, then return to it. If not, I'll come over and we can swing the Culture Club together.

Dollars and Dimes

On an almost daily basis, I read stories about significant expenditures on all sorts of projects. It might be a new runway for an airport, an expanded distribution center for a major retailer, or a state-of-the-art research complex. Even when the projects are completed at or near budget, the projected return on the investment is rarely realized.

This expense vs. return disparity is not restricted to capital projects. More often than not, medium-sized expenditures for things like product development, marketing, and staffing also lead to overspending.

If you review the situation carefully, you will find that the cost overruns come from one, often modest, decision at a time, rather than from a sweeping major change in the overall plan. In the grand scheme of things, these decisions will seem like just a few dimes here and there rather than "real money."

It happens quickly. A key member of the project team requests that two additional, unbudgeted people come on a trip to San Francisco. The costs go up. An opportunity to buy specially priced furniture and fixtures—more than is required—for the new offices up on the tenth floor seems like a good idea at the time. The costs go up.

Marketing decides on running ads in five industry magazines rather than the previously agreed upon three, to ensure broader exposure. The costs go up.

A well-qualified candidate surfaces unexpectedly, for a position that doesn't exist on this project, and "we just got to hire her." The costs go up. Even these good decisions can quickly drive up the price while not necessarily increasing the quality of the project.

Chances are those two additional people, that extra furniture, those additional ads, and even that well-qualified candidate really aren't necessary to complete your project in an effective and efficient matter. If the project plan was built properly, everything that was required was already in it. These new, different, even wonderful items and people, no matter how attractive, are most likely not required.

Yes, adding those resources, buying that furniture, or hiring that great candidate would be wonderful.

But every one of these situations is an example of some sort of cost creep. It could be scope creep, headcount creep, expense creep, or time creep. Any way you look at it, it is still creepy. All of these actions would result in "jacking up" costs and there is no way to "jack down" those costs once they are in place.

The Common Sense Approach here is to spend absolutely every dollar necessary for your project and your company to be successful, but not to spend a single dime more.

Fail

There are many ridiculous—some might say dangerous—management mantras in the business world today. Perhaps the worst among them is, "Failure Is Not an Option." While nobody wants to fail, stating that failure is not an option is just absurd.

Of course failure is an option. When I hear that phrase, I wonder if the person saying it understands that, in this context, "option" simply means a possible outcome. Failure is a possible outcome and therefore failure *is* an option.

Beyond the linguistic absurdity, the very idea that management never sees failure as an option is a business absurdity. Do they only want to attempt things at which it is impossible to fail? How will that lead to game-changing developments, breakthrough products, and the ability to enter new markets?

Have these managers become so afraid of making a mistake, of **failing**, that they will not take any meaningful risks? Have they become so comfortable in the status quo that they have lost the will to experiment or invent?

Failure **is** an option, perhaps even a desired one, for at least it demonstrates that the company is trying to do something of consequence. Without continued experimentation, a company will grow stagnant and then become irrelevant, while others around them are failing away and adjusting each time they fail.

Albert Einstein once said, "If we knew what it was we were doing, it would not be called research, would it?" It is that courage to try, fail, learn, try again, maybe fail some more, that leads to true innovation, medical cures, space flight, and market-defining products.

Many of today's most respected and profitable companies have failed plenty of times. Amazon and Walmart have failed at attempts to enter certain international markets. Apple has failed on almost as many product launches as they have succeeded (think of The Lisa and The Newton.)

3M, a decades-long Fortune 100 company, failed so badly when it first started that it went bankrupt once and was on the edge of bankruptcy a second time, all in its first five years.

The Common Sense Approach here is to find the right balance between failure and success in your firm. Keep pushing for greatness. If you are never failing, you are not trying hard enough to thrive. Failing every once in a while is a great way to ensure that your whole business doesn't fail.

Family Business

In my corporate career I've had the honor of being an employee of many family businesses. In fact, I built significant careers at two of them. And now in my consulting practice I regularly provide advice to family businesses. I've seen several grow and be smoothly transitioned to the appropriate people within the next generation. Sadly, I've also seen several fail during that transition, or fail because of the lack of transition.

Through all of that experience, I've learned many lessons. Chief among them is that for a family business to truly thrive, the emphasis must be balanced between family and business. It is critical that personnel and promotion decisions **not** be made simply because this person or that person is in the family. It is equally critical that family matters be considered while business decisions are made.

In my consulting work I've been called into many family firms specifically because I was **not** a member of the family. When this happens, I serve as a sort of arbiter to help the firm balance family and business. As an outsider, both from the family and from the business, it is a lot easier for me to help in setting that balance.

Just because the founding generation, or the generation currently running the business, has children or siblings, that doesn't automatically mean those people are qualified for senior jobs in the firm. Likewise, just because someone is a member of the family they should not be automatically disqualified for a position with the firm.

While one solution or the other may seem like the best thing for the business *or* for the family, you must view these situations through the lens of what is best for the business *and* for the family. The boss's son doesn't have to be the best person for the job, but he absolutely needs to be qualified. Similarly, just because the best qualified person is the founder's granddaughter shouldn't mean she shouldn't get the job because of family fears or bickering.

There are often situations when there is a mostly qualified family member who is not quite ready to take that next step. Having a person outside the family installed as a placeholder to support and mentor that family member until they are ready is an excellent solution.

Your family will most likely endure well past the end of its control of the business. Are your feelings about Uncle Billy strong enough to risk the future of the business? Is your desire for business success strong enough to risk your family relationships? You don't want the family to destroy the business and you don't want the business to destroy the family.

The Common Sense Approach here is to strike and maintain the balance between the family matters and the business issues. Family is family. Business is business. A family business is both.

Flight

Flying has always *seemed* to be a complex and magical thing. The truth is that flying is a *simple* and scientific thing.

Throughout the ages, humans have always tried to find a way to fly. For the first 10,000 years or so, those attempts led to negative outcomes, often ending in death. All of those attempts, by the brave, the wise, and the mad were tragically based on a misunderstanding of how flight actually happens.

It was only in the last 2,000 years or so that there was any measure of success, with simple things like kites and then balloons. Even Leonardo da Vinci was unable to solve this problem. Somewhere around 1901 (the date is still in some dispute) humans were able to have sustained, controlled, powered flight.

As I said earlier, this delay stemmed from a misunderstanding of how flight works. Rather than putting all of that effort into amazingly complex solutions for how people *thought* flight worked, they could have put the effort into replicating how flight *actually works*.

The reality is that flight is very simple to understand, but hard to execute. The simple part is that whenever the speed of air moving below an object is faster than the air moving above it, that object flies.

You can try this at home. Just grab a piece of paper, lay it on a flat surface, and then blow under it. Your breath will be moving at a speed greater than the still air above the paper and the paper will fly as long as you keep blowing beneath it.

A major component of the work I do, both as a speaker and as a consultant, is to help demystify the *seemingly* complex. My experience has taught me that most people want their problems to be complex and difficult. This makes it okay if they struggle to deal with something new, like a technology advance or a change in market conditions.

Much more often than not, we find that the actual problem is not complex. More often than not, the solution is also not complex. However, and here is where we really earn our money, getting the client to commit to the changes required to address the actual cause of the problem is very complex.

These changes—be they operational, financial, technical, or directional—are what make the execution so complex. Even presented with the facts of problem, cause, and solution, many businesses will not exercise the will to make the required changes.

The Common Sense Approach here is to bring in some fresh eyes, look until you find the *actual* cause of your problem, and then do whatever is appropriate to address it. If you do those things, then you will be flying high.

Free is Not an F Word

A very interesting, yet very dangerous thing has happened in business the past several years; companies have become completely mesmerized over the idea of *free* as a price. Some businesspeople love *free* as a price and some businesspeople think *free* is a four-letter F word.

Well, the reality of the situation is that both camps are wrong.

Perhaps the best examples are what most people think of free as a business model are Google and Facebook. Well, I'm here to tell you that the only ones getting anything free where those two firms are concerned are, well, Google and Facebook.

You see, every time you use the Google search tool, Gmail, Facebook, or any other of the what-appears-to-be-free services from these two, you are actually *paying* them with your eyeballs, your keystrokes, and your preference data. You are contributing for *free,* and Google and Facebook are making a fortune off your free labor.

Oh, it sure seems like it is free, but by using these services you are actually contributing a massive amount of user search and preference data that gets turned into the ad-targeting services they sell for real money to companies all over the world.

Google and Facebook didn't take in over $70 billion in sales last year because they have lots of inventive ways to represent the letters in their name above the search box. So the people who love using Google and Facebook for *free* are dead wrong about what they are actually paying.

The people who think *free* is a four-letter F word are also wrong, just not as much.

Free as a price, either all alone or with the hope of making a sale later, is really an F'ed-up idea, so they are right about that part.

However, *free*, as part of much larger strategy, *a la* Google and Facebook, is a beautiful thing to behold.

The Common Sense Approach here is for your business to focus on providing a valuable service that people are willing to pay for and not just giving things away so people will like you. *Free* isn't a real price, but it can be a valuable part of a real strategy.

Free Time

Now, I don't want any of you to be alarmed or disappointed, but there will be math in this chapter. To make it a bit worse, this is time math.

It seems that everybody I know feels they are pressed for time, out of time, or trying to find ways to save time. Well, the good news is that I'm here to tell you that there are over six weeks of time right here, just ready for the taking.

Okay, so here comes the math part.

There are 52 weeks in a year. There are five regular work days in a week. If you multiply those five days by those 52 weeks, you get a total of 260 days. By reclaiming just one hour a day, you would have 260 more hours. Using an average of 40 hours per week, those 260 hours would give you 6½ weeks' worth of time.

A simple recap. An hour a day, on each work day, yields those 6½ weeks of reclaimed time.

Earlier, I said the time was just there for the taking. The key word here is *taking*. While the price of this free time is $0, you do still need to *do* something to take it back. The thing you need to do is exercise the discipline required to say "no" to things that are stealing your time.

You need to say "no" to meetings whose topics could have been handled in a simple email. You need to say "no" to reading weekly status reports on projects that don't require weekly updating. You need to say "no" to searching for more information than is actually required to make your decisions.

These are the three key mistakes that almost everyone makes. No doubt, you can easily think of others that apply just to you.

These wasted activities are the time thieves that you are allowing to steal your 6½ weeks. Rather than taking cash, they are taking minutes, hours, days, and weeks. You have plenty of time; you are just letting these thieves take it from you.

Wasted time is one of the main economic drags in business today. As the speed of business continues to increase, wasted time becomes more expensive than ever.

It feels like you need more time. But if you do the math, you will learn that you have way more time than you think you do. You need to reposition your thinking to protect your time like you protect your other resources.

The Common Sense Approach here is for you to *pay* closer attention to how you are *spending* your time. Take better control over your schedule. Take back those 6½ weeks. After all, time is money.

Game On

I'm going to encourage all y'all to get your game on! Video Gaming, always a strong market, has become huge. The most recent figures estimate world-wide video gaming revenue at $2 trillion. And it's not all teenagers playing in the basement; the average age of today's video gamer is 31. In addition to recreational game play, there are not one but two professional leagues for gaming; the Professional Gaming League and Major League Gaming.

Beyond video gaming, board games are also huge. This year's *Internationale Spieltage* drew more than 160,000 fans to Essen, Germany. Let's just say the business of gaming is booming.

Games and gaming have also become integrated into much of what we do. Think about things like frequent flyer programs, credit card rewards, and even the annual McDonald's Monopoly game. Those ideas are driving significant business results by applying the same type of level-up processes used in games. When you add in mobile and Facebook games like *Candy Crush* and *Words with Friends*, it looks like everybody is playing along.

Games are also becoming a critical component in addressing the needs of our K-12 and college students. Game-based learning is a huge growth area. Basically, games and gaming are showing up everywhere.

In my consulting practice, I regularly work with companies that are trying to attract workers *and* customers from the gaming generation. Part of my work is a review of how and when gaming would fit within their company. The fit could be a new product or a change in a business process. By helping the client understand the gaming fit for their business, I allow them to obtain and retain those workers and customers.

When a societal factor grows as large as gaming and that same factor is generating trillions of dollars of revenue, it is time for businesses to take notice or risk being left on the sidelines.

There are a growing number of products and services available today that are directly integrating gaming practices into regular business functions like HR and marketing. The employees who are going to take your business into the future expect gaming to be a normal part of the work. Your future customers do, too.

The Common Sense Approach here is to understand the impact that games and gaming can have on your business and then make the adjustments to capitalize on it. Basically, learn the rules and get into the game.

How Much

A key challenge in business is knowing when you know enough to make an informed decision. As is discussed in the *Traffic Lights* chapter, waiting until you know "everything" and thereby never moving forward is clearly not the right answer.

So how do you know? There is no textbook answer, but I've found the following process to be reliable.

Picture an old-school weighing scale, the kind with two sides that are kept in balance by having an equal weight on each plate.

Picture one side being full of pebbles that represent the business challenge or opportunity. This is the Problem side. The pebbles represent the many facets of the problem, since there is never just one big issue. These facets could be people, technology advances, regulations, competitors or whatever is causing the situation. Since there is now a lot of weight on this one side, the scale is out of balance.

Now shift your attention to the other side of the scale, the one that represents what you need to know. This is the Knowledge side. The pebbles on this side represent the many things you need to know before you can move forward. Believe it or not, there are already some pebbles on this side. This is true because you already know things. You know your budget numbers, your staffing levels, your organization's skills *and* skills gaps. You also know some things about the competition, pending legislation, and upcoming demographic changes.

The next step is to remove pebbles from the Problem side. Very carefully inspect those pebbles to

47

ensure they are truly aspects of the problem rather than just fears or worries. Already, the scale moves closer to balance.

Now, determine what *can be known* in direct relation to the remaining problem pebbles. From this point, for each thing you learn you add a pebble to the Knowledge side. As soon as the scales balance, you are ready to take whatever is the appropriate action.

Don't allow yourself and your organization to become distracted by the desire to know more than is required. You can always keep learning, but you can't always wait to make the next business decision.

The Common Sense Approach here is to treat your information gathering with a specific and measurable target in mind rather than just constantly collecting knowledge. Once you master this, your organization will be balanced and ready to go.

Insanity

Just about everyone knows the quote, "The definition of insanity is doing the same thing over and over again and expecting a different result." Well, I have a minor modification to that quote that reflects what I see happening regularly in the business world. The modified quote is, "The definition of **business** insanity is doing the same thing over and over again and expecting the **same** result."

Business leaders often expect to be able to just do the same things they have been doing all along, without regard for the ever-increasing speed of change or adjusting to a more tech-savvy and mobile customer base.

The business news is full of reports about long-standing firms that have not adapted to changing market conditions and are now struggling mightily to just survive. A quick list of examples includes Macy's, Radio Shack, Blackberry, and Adidas.

More often than not, these businesses grow stagnant or, worse, begin to shrink, and then disappear from market prominence. A long-standing record of excellent performance is not to be dismissed. After all, the business got to 80 or 100 years old by doing things the right way. Keeping those core elements while exploring new and different processes or markets would be the best blend. The reasons for wanting to do the same thing over and over again are usually hidden behind the ideas of a *history of strength*, the *power of our brand*, or the notion that *We Do Things the Company X Way*.

I say "hidden behind" because the true reason these businesses do not change is that they don't know how. The urge to invent has long since been overcome by the short-term drive for profits. The willingness to take risks has been replaced by risk mitigation departments. The deep connection to the customer has been replaced by automated customer management centers.

The rate of change has never been faster in human history. Worse yet, that rate will continue to increase. The barriers to entry in most markets have been lowered so far as to barely exist. With some basic web tools and a PayPal account just about anybody can open up an e-Commerce site tomorrow morning to sell just about anything to just about anyone.

Yet, most people running businesses today are moving even more slowly than they did ten years ago. More meetings than ever are taking place. The number of customer surveys and the amount of market research have grown to epidemic proportions.

Businesses aren't taking risks, they aren't hiring new and different thinkers, they aren't investing in R&D, and they aren't learning new and different ways to do things. They are primarily doing what they have always done and expecting the **same** result.

The Common Sense Approach here is for businesses to constantly be looking at fresh approaches, new products, and new opportunities as they figure out how to do things differently. Keep the core elements of your success and replace the rest.

Internet of Nothing

I'm starting to wonder if I'll ever be able to get through another day without hearing the phrase, "The Internet of Things." The idea that everything from my car to my treadmill should be connected to the Internet seems to be something that everyone needs to report on several times *every day*.

Is this all really necessary? I'm not sure I want my toaster, my refrigerator, and my scale to communicate and then cooperate to stop me from having a wonderful late-night snack while I'm writing the next episode of Common Sense Comments.

In an attempt to bring all this talk to a sensible level, I'd like you to consider the "Internet of Nothing". Yep, nothing. That's right, take a minute and think about how you would run your business if you had no connection to the internet.

Don't panic, I'm not actually going to make it happen. I just want you to think about it. The talking heads will pressure you many times a day with the notion that everything **needs** to be connected to everything else. To what end, I ask you?

I am a technologist and strategist. I appreciate the opportunity in having your suppliers, your warehouse, and your delivery trucks all flowing with real-time inventory updates. I've worked on some of those projects. The possibilities of faster service, better resource management, new sales, and higher productivity are all right there before you.

What I recommend you do is start from the Internet of Nothing and work with your senior team to see what pieces of your business **should** be connected rather than what pieces of your business **could** be connected.

What good is it for you to know that a retail customer of yours is out of inventory if you have no ready plan to replenish it? Are you really better off knowing that your supplier in Colesville, MD, has the parts you urgently need if you don't have a process to immediately order them?

Remember, you are starting by having nothing connected at all. Dig deep to really understand what your business and your customers need, find the appropriate points of connection and then connect them. Stay balanced during this process. Understand that changes and investments will be required to put all these connections to their proper use.

The Common Sense Approach here is for you to review everything that you, your customers, and your suppliers are doing and then make the appropriate connections happen. The Internet is waiting for you, but not for long.

Just Sales, No Products

There are businesses out there, some of them very large, that are making a ton of sales without actually selling any products. It seems unreal, but I assure you that it is indeed real. They have no products, but they are providing valuable services.

I'm taking about firms like Uber, Alibaba, Airbnb, and eBay. These firms and others like them have completely upended their markets. And then, once they build some momentum in their initial markets, these companies quickly begin to impact other, adjacent markets.

Uber, and its competitors, began by disrupting the traditional cab service in major cities. They have no cabs, but they provide millions of rides a year. Now these app-based car services are starting to take business from rental-car companies, too. In fact, a small but growing number of consumers are not buying cars at all, since the ease of summoning a car only when you need one has made life without car ownership plausible.

Airbnb, without owning any real estate or having any hotel licensing agreements or experience, is facilitating the rental of rooms all over the country and all over the world. Beyond their impact on the hotel/motel chains, Airbnb and other firms like it are also having an impact on the short-term apartment and house rental markets, since more clients are interested in using them for those types of stays as well.

Alibaba and eBay, without having any inventory, are connecting people who have stuff to sell with people who want to buy that stuff. eBay's initial play appeared to be a threat only to garage sales and flea markets. Once buyers got used to the idea of checking eBay for more than just things like a ticket from a 1978 Springsteen concert, more and more sellers added more and more merchandise. These sites currently list plenty of new merchandise that can be purchased without the auction process. Now the threat is to retail stores, shopping malls, and even other e-Commerce sites.

In each of these new economy scenarios, and no doubt in new ones being developed as you read this chapter, the company is offering a service and not a product. The service is actually being offered on both ends of the transaction.

The customer is offered the convenience of a centralized and easy-to-use site which offers millions of products and services from thousands of merchants in locations all over the world. All this without having to go into a store, let alone having to find a parking space. The seller gets the opportunity to have their products and services discovered by more customers than they could ever imagine with a physical location, a toll-free number, or on their direct stand-alone website.

With the current state of technology, to say nothing of what will surface in the next 18 months, service-only offerings are redefining the way shopping and shipping occur.

The Common Sense Approach here is for you to understand, right now, how such a disruptive force is impacting your business, and then make the changes necessary to ensure you can ride this wave of innovation rather than be drowned by it.

Mousetrap

There is an old saying in business that goes something like; "*Build a better mousetrap and the world will beat a path to your door.*" Well, I'm here to tell you that isn't necessarily so.

Some things can be modified, perhaps, but that doesn't necessarily make them better. Products can be made lighter, cheaper, easier to install–all modifications of one type of another, but are they really better?

Let's take a look at the very mousetrap itself. In 1894, William C. Hooker patented the very basic, spring-loaded mousetrap. Beyond some simple safety (for the humans, at least) modifications made by John Mast in 1899, that very same mousetrap is in use today.

That basic trap, known today by the Victor trademark, still sells by the millions each year. You see, that product is an irreducibly complex item. It is as simple as it can be and still functions. In essence, you can't build a better one.

Of course, that doesn't stop people from trying. There are many firms out there, including the folks at Victor, who keep trying to come up with a better mousetrap. Design changes, new materials, poisons, even sound waves. Modifications, yes; improvements, no. The plane wood base with a metal spring still solves the problem better.

Imagine if all that energy, talent, and money was spent on solving a problem that needed solving.

In my consulting practice I do a significant amount of product strategy work. Oftentimes, I get the call after a few failed attempts to realize a strategy, and so the job becomes a rescue mission. While these are difficult assignments, I do really enjoy them.

Typically, we begin with an open and honest discussion of what *customer* problem the company was trying to solve with this new product. Usually this leads to the realization that the team was trying to solve a *company* problem and not a customer problem. From there we can find a new target, build a new strategy, and start again.

Too many companies today are attempting to make modifications to existing product or service ideas rather than truly challenging themselves to design something new.

Businesses in general have become too risk averse and shortsighted to be willing to take the big chances required to make the big advances they are seeking. Making incremental changes, especially to products that already work very well, is no way to grow a company.

In order to thrive in the twenty-first century, we must all embrace bolder thinking, take greater risks, and truly push ourselves to make breakthrough products.

The Common Sense Approach here is to find customer problems that have not yet been solved and apply your resources against solving those problems. After all, you don't want to get trapped in old thinking.

Mustang

The year is 1961. A man named Lido, about a year into his new job, has a vision which will become one of the greatest products in the history of his industry.

The man is better known as Lee and by his last name, Iacocca. This new job was not at Chrysler, but as VP and General Manager at Ford Motor Company. His vision led to the Ford Mustang.

The genius of Iacocca's vision was more about the specifics rather than some undefined dream. Lee didn't set out to build the fastest car on the market. He didn't set out to build the cheapest car. His interest wasn't about building a large family car. Iacocca didn't care about building the car with the greatest street appeal.

Lee's vision, his true master work, was to focus on the blend of all four of these factors. Before anyone put pencil to paper, he saw a car *strong enough* in all four areas.

Lee felt Ford needed a car that was fast enough to appeal to men, roomy enough to handle a baby-boomer family, inexpensive enough to appeal to the masses, and good-looking enough to still be cool.

Nothing like this had ever been done before in the history of cars. Ford's leadership, meaning the Ford family themselves, backed this plan, and the rest is automotive history.

Iacocca's seemingly impossible and almost heretical blending of different design concepts and feature sets made this car something totally special and totally different.

The Mustang, in all its many variations over the years, is one of the most recognizable and successful car models of all time. The Mustang remains a top seller today, more than 50 years after its introduction.

In my consulting work, I spend a fair amount of time in product design and concept meetings. Whatever the industry, from software to content creation to conveyor belt systems, my client often feels they know what the customer wants and how to follow the established path of how things "must be done" to satisfy those wants.

By injecting some alternative thoughts into the design and development process, I help my clients expand their overall strategy.

By taking a broader view and including multiple facets of the customers' needs, companies can build better overall products rather than delivering ones that are very strong in one area and weak in most others.

The Common Sense Approach here is to look more deeply and broadly into your customers' needs and then expand your company's ability to address those needs. Do that and you'll be firing on all cylinders.

News

Extra, extra, this just in: Newspapers are alive and well! Yes, I know it is 2016. I also know that just about everybody else is telling you that digital has made print irrelevant. Trust me, this is not the case.

Newspapers as a business model are not dead. However, inefficient and poorly run newspapers are dead. Papers that are run by people who do not understand the service they offer are dead. As in any other business segment, newspapers that have lost their focus are certainly dead.

The opposite is also true. Newspapers that understand and stay focused on the value they add to the reader are OK. Newspapers that stay local and provide value to the local community are OK.

You don't have to believe just me. You can check with the best investor in the history of the world, Warren Buffett. The Oracle of Omaha continues to be bullish on newspapers. Through Berkshire Hathaway, Buffet owns almost 50 different papers in an operation that spans ten states.

This not a situation where Buffett is holding on to old-school properties for sentimental reasons. In fact, Berkshire just added another paper to the stable a few months ago.

Far from attempting to build a sprawling global media empire, each of Berkshire's newspapers exists within the narrow and unique markets it serves directly. They vary in size from 580 readers at the Tulsa Business & Legal News to newspapers in Richmond, Buffalo, and Omaha that each have circulations approaching or exceeding 100,000.

All of these papers focus on the combination of reporting on the specific things their readers want to read and offering effective classified ads. Sexy or snazzy it is not, but steady and profitable it certainly is.

Contrast this with a paper like the Chicago Tribune and you can understand why some papers fail and others succeed. The Tribune, a once-powerful newspaper, completely lost its way through a series of debt-laden purchases of other media firms, and also by buying non-media things like the Chicago Cubs.

All of these activities increased their debt load and most of them also lost money. Along the way, the paper forgot its place in the community, slashed its costs–including laying off many quality journalists–and generally made a mess of things. Today, a shell of what it once was, the battered and badly run *Trib* is in a fight to not be acquired by Gannett Publishing.

The Common Sense Approach here is to understand the business you are actually in rather than engage in some grand fantasy. Run your business as efficiently and effectively as possible while providing services your customers need and value. Keep your eye on the target. If you do that, your business will surely be front-page news.

Not an Opera Singer

During my many decades here on planet Earth, I have seen and done many things. I have visited 48 of the 50 U.S. states and five of the seven continents. I have held many jobs, played many sports, been married for over a quarter of a century, and, with the incredible help of my lovely bride, raised three amazing sons.

I have written two books; one of them even hit #1 on Amazon. I have advised companies in about a dozen different countries. I have given speeches to groups that varied in size from just one of my sons up to a ballroom full of people with a live stream audience beyond them. I have been called Dad, Granddad, husband, son, uncle, nephew, player, coach, stock-boy, programmer, co-worker, boss, and CEO. You see, I have been, and still am, many things.

However, one thing I am not is an opera singer. While this should be obvious, especially to those of you who know me and have heard me sing, it is still important for me to state it out loud and to recognize and accept that I am not an opera singer. It is true today and will be true forever.

The important part of the statement is not the opera singer part, but the acknowledgement that I am not, and cannot, be everything and do everything. It would be just as true for me to say I am not a pro golfer or a bass player. You see, a big piece of knowing who we are is understanding who we are not. Knowing our weaknesses at least as well as we know our strengths is critical to overall success.

By recognizing, accepting, and being willing to say out loud that I am not an opera singer, a pro golfer, or a bass player, I demonstrate that I know my limits and I also open myself up to the fact that if I require skills, experiences, and qualities that I do not possess, I need to surround myself with those who do possess them.

Too many business people today think that because they are smart, that they had a great idea, or that they have had previous successes, they can do anything and everything required to help their company thrive. One person simply can't be the whole company. This has been true since the dawn of the age of specialization, and in today's world it is so far from true that it is almost laughable.

The skills required to be truly successful today are so varied, the hours required to keep up with today's pace of business are so long, the pace of change is so fast, and the amount and variety of technology platforms that are necessary to stay informed and communicate with your customers are so numerous, no single person stands a chance of doing it all.

Regardless of how well rounded and experienced you are, there are still plenty of gaps in your overall portfolio. Even if you somehow achieve mastery in all the skills required to make your company successful, you cannot go without sleep and you cannot be in more than one place at a time. Do what you are best at doing. Hire and empower the other people necessary to complement your skills and help your company thrive.

The Common Sense Approach here is to recognize who you are and who you are not. Then build around you a team of people with a wide variety of attributes and interests so that you can be a real leader and run a great company. Focus on being you. Find the right complementary team and let them be themselves, too.

Oxygen

This is about how your business can best help others. The others could be co-workers, marketplace partners, customers, or investors. It doesn't matter who the other person is since this is about how *you* can help.

I take you now to the safety briefing demonstration that all airplane travelers can probably recite in their sleep. Perhaps because we have all heard it a zillion times, nobody actually listens to it any more.

During those briefings, there is a whole section on the "unlikely event" of a change in cabin pressure. I'll pause for a second while you get there in your mind.

Okay, we are losing cabin pressure: that is important. This affects the oxygen level in the cabin: that is important. A mask drops from the ceiling: that is important.

And now for the super-important part: if you are travelling with someone else, *put your mask on first* then go to help them. This is because if you are partially comprised, you can't be fully helpful. *Put your mask on first* so that you have the oxygen and therefore the mental awareness you need to be of optimal assistance.

A lot of my speaking engagements, regardless of the main topic, end up including Q&A around how to manage change, especially in times of crisis such as market upheaval or technology disruption. As a strategy consultant, I do bring oxygen to my clients.

So let's transition this oxygen mask situation to the everyday world. If you are not maintaining the health of your business–sales, expenses, and R&D investments–how much help can you really be to others?

If your company can't turn a profit, how are you going to be able to help your customers, employees, suppliers, and shareholders? If there is a cash flow or investment-level problem, how can you respond if you have no cash?

If you can't keep your finances clear, your staff rested, and your company spirit strong, how much help can you offer your co-workers, your supply chain, or your end users? If you are already tired, how will you maintain the stamina needed to carry the load for others?

You need to understand that helping your business first is not being selfish. By helping your business first, you put yourself in a position to help more people for longer periods of time.

The Common Sense Approach here is to make sure your business is in the best possible shape so that you can give–and keep giving–assistance when the need arises. Without oxygen, you can't breathe and you can't help.

Paper Cuts

About ten years ago I was sitting in a conference room with the heads of a group of companies that did about a half-billion dollars' worth of annual business. During that meeting, the president of the entire group asked each company head to come to the next meeting and detail how they would get by using half as much paper within their operation.

It was one of the best resource management lessons I had ever seen and it remains so to this day. No grand proclamations. No teams or themes. Just go and do it.

This request led to a robust discussion about how each of the companies used paper. Reports being printed that nobody ever read, marketing flyers that never got mailed, and so on and so on. You see, the paperless office is one of the greatest myths in business.

Even today, when I meet with my consulting clients, we talk about this story. Making businesses more efficient, and therefore more profitable, is a central part of the work I do. A quick double-check of those "automatic" spending categories can yield some nice piles of cash.

Perhaps the best part of the whole story is that the reports never actually got written. Truth be told, there was never any intention to have them written. The point was never paper. The group president could have said "half the gasoline" or "half the hotel rooms." The point was to get the presidents thinking differently about how their companies spend.

In most companies today, there are significant areas of expense reduction that go unnoticed because they seem like minor matters. The interesting twist about the "half the paper" story is that it got the presidents to reset their spending mindsets rather than just looking for budget items to slash. By setting the conceptual target of half the paper, that group president also set the stage for deeper thinking about expenses.

By working with the department heads to understand the needs behind the spending, business leaders often find extraordinary savings in the ordinary way the business flows.

The Common Sense Approach here is for businesses to rethink the way they spend money, especially on the everyday things such as paper, to ensure that all their spending is applied against what the business truly needs.

Paperbacks

There is so much disruption going on in business today it can be hard to tell who the entrenched players are and who are the disruptors. The disruption can be within an industry, such as bookstores or taxi cabs, or across something even broader, such as shipping packages or publishing.

Perhaps the most recognizable name in bookstore disruption is Amazon. As it happens, Amazon also controls one of the most recognizable names in the disruption of the publishing process, the Kindle eBook reader.

While it is certainly true that Amazon has disrupted both publishing and retail, it is hardly the first firm to do either. Each of those markets has been disrupted, and with great regularity, since the beginning.

Rather than make this a history lecture, I'll just give you a quick example of some previous disruptions. From 1939, we have a *Publishers Weekly* article from the American Booksellers Convention that states some *"Reckless* publisher" was going to release *paper-back* books! Books would now cost less than a dollar. Clearly that was the *end of publishing*. Of course, similar claims were made when Amazon released the Kindle and eBooks were set to *destroy* publishing. And yet, great books continue to be written, printed, and sold all over the place.

A similar story can be told about the *end of the retail store* from 1956, when Southdale Center, the first enclosed mall, opened in the Minneapolis-St. Paul area. Clearly, this would kill the regular store. Of course, that spawned all sorts of shopping experiences, large and small, all across the world. Then came e-Commerce. Once again, *stores* were doomed. Well, that isn't happening. In fact, web retailers, including Amazon, are now opening physical stores. Other online-only outlets like Warby Parker, Blue Nile, and Bonobos are opening physical stores to allow customers to do things you can't do online line such as touch the merchandise and try it on.

I've given many talks on this topic including one that focuses on how the firm responsible for Borders going out of business was Borders and not Amazon. While Borders remained focused on being a book*store*, Amazon was focused on being a book*seller*. Borders placed its needs above those of the customer.

You see, it is not the new thing, the cool thing, the cheap thing, or even what appears to be the easy thing that makes a business successful. It is the intimate relationship a business has with its customers that makes a business successful.

The Common Sense Approach here is to dig until you truly understand the unique relationship you have with your customers. Once you understand that, you can maintain it. Make sure not to let anything disrupt that relationship, and chances are, nobody will be able to disrupt your business.

Publix

This chapter is the first Common Sense Comments company spotlight. The featured company is the grocery store chain, Publix.

I chose Publix for two key reason. First, it is turning a nice profit in one of the most difficult markets in America—grocery stores. Second, it has an amazing focus on its customers and the front-line employees who serve them. That twin focus—not low prices, not expense reductions, not the Internet— makes the firm so profitable.

Publix has just over 1,100 stores, all of which are in the Southeast. I've been in some of these stores. They are, at once, nothing special and totally amazing. If you get to that part of the country, do drop in and experience the Publix difference. You will be pleased, perhaps even amazed.

As I said, Publix operates in one of the most difficult markets in America. Against competitors that are much larger (think Walmart and Kroger), inventory that starts to spoil almost as soon as it's received (think produce, dairy, and meat), and a notoriously difficult staffing environment (the industry averages a 65% turnover rate), Publix just keeps getting better.

To make things even more interesting, Publix is an employee-owned, privately held company, and has been since 1974. In fact, at over $30 billion in annual sales, it is the world's largest employee-owned company.

Most of the things Publix does put it at the polar opposite of what the Ivy League MBA types suggest. Publix regularly hires, trains, and promotes staff with no college education. Employees are eligible for raises every six months. Publix focuses on creating happy and loyal employees first who in turn create happy and loyal customers. By treating its employees so well, Publix creates a store-full of staff who then treat the customers with respect and with a full-service attitude

So what is the secret?

How do they do it?

Can our company do it too?

Basically, the truth is that the secret is not really a secret. Publix is very open with how they recruit, train, and retain their employees. By the way, the voluntary turnover rate at Publix is 5%, which is about 90% below the industry average.

Publix "does it" by actually and truly striving for the same two goals that its founder, George W. Jenkins, started with way back in 1930. Those two goals are:

1) To create the world's most pleasurable shopping experience
2) To create the world's best workplace

So, can your company do it too? Hmm, I don't know. Publix does lay it all out there for you to see if you are willing to open your eyes and do the work.

The Common Sense Approach here is to study Publix, actually visit its stores, and learn from its approach. If you are willing to do that, things should really check out for you.

Resources

In all my years as a strategy consultant, I cannot think of a single situation in which the client said they had plenty of resources. Actually, I don't remember a client saying they had even enough resources. It seems that every company in the world is resource constrained.

This is true whether I'm working with a pre-revenue startup or a multi-billion dollar, multinational corporation. It is true in a tinkerer's garage and even in the Googleplex.

Regardless of the type of company, the type of project, or the marketplace being served, there are always resource constraints. Even where it would seem as though a company would have virtually unlimited cash to throw at a project, there are still resource shortages around time and talent.

Too many people spend too much time either complaining about or worrying about resources. At some stage in the conversation, I just want to say, "resources, *schmesources*." The reality is there is always pressure on resources. The challenge of the business leader is to determine and set the corporate priorities and then allow the appropriate resources to be deployed against those priorities.

It is never the amount of resources that causes business problems. It is the misapplication of those resources that leads to corporate waste and missed opportunities.

Starting a project before resources are committed to it is not the same thing as not having enough resources for that project. The core element here is balance. Balancing the threats facing your business, the opportunities available to your business, and the resources you have within your business is the real challenge.

As a strategy consultant, I regularly work with clients to help them with this balancing act. The main issue is to determine what is truly needed by the business rather than what various departments within the company want.

The Common Sense Approach here is to set and then **support** only the projects that are key to your company's success and survival. If a project doesn't fit one of those categories, then don't give it any resources. You should focus your resources where they are truly needed and not allow your company's resources to be depleted by things that don't move it forward.

Revolution

Revolutions can be exciting and liberating. They can also be frightening and deadly. Regardless of what else happens, a true revolution brings rapid and significant change.

This is true whether the revolution is in a country, a culture, or an entire category of business. Typically, we use words like *industrial revolution* when we talk about business. During each of these revolutions, all of the conditions I mentioned earlier come to pass.

While the word "industrial" tends to bring to mind things like mills, machines, and railroads, this is too narrow a view. There are many industries in the business world and so the phrase *industrial revolution* needs to accommodate all industries.

For this discussion, I'd like you to consider that we are firmly in the fourth major industrial revolution. Very quickly, the first three were:

1780s — advances in machine production, steam engine power, and railroads

1870s — mass production, electric power, and assembly line factories

1960s — automated production, consumer electronics, and computers

And right now we are in the fourth, with things like robotic production, data analytics, and artificial intelligence becoming part of all we do.

As you will have noticed, the revolutions are coming more frequently. As you will have also noticed, each revolution has production as a driver.

Each of these revolutions, including the current one, has created great tumult and provided great opportunity. The tumult comes from the twin factors of not being prepared for the revolution and being resistant to the resulting changes. The opportunity comes from the twin factors of watching for the signs of the revolution and adapting to the resulting changes.

Some companies, like IBM, drive and power these revolutions. Founded way back in 1911 as The Computing-Tabulating-Recording Company, IBM has been a key player in the last two revolutions.

Some companies, like Kodak and Xerox, were overwhelmed by these revolutions, despite having developed some of the very technologies that ended up driving them into irrelevance. In Kodak's case, it was the digital camera in 1975. And for Xerox it was the computer mouse which their board didn't appreciate and made the engineers share with Apple.

One of my key roles as a strategy consultant is to help firms see the signs of change early enough so that they can prepare for, or perhaps even participate in, the next revolution.

By bringing outside thinking into my client companies, I am in a position to help them see things they would otherwise have missed as they focused on internal matters.

The Common Sense Approach here is to watch and listen for the sounds and signs of revolution. Align yourself and your operations so that you are in position to ride the wave forward. As everybody knows, revolutions never go backward.

Sledgehammer

Sometimes a sledgehammer is the right tool.

Tools have been with humankind for a few million years. Business tools are, admittedly, a bit more recent. However, the rate of change and the proliferation of business tools are staggering. In today's business world, there are multiple tools for just about every function. We have marketing tools, targeting tools, sales tools, and inventory tools. You name it, there is a tool, or an app, for that.

The point that often gets missed in business today, especially when dealing with technology, is that sometimes the right tool is an old-school tool like a sledgehammer. You see, just because something can be done with automation, doesn't mean it *should* be done with automation.

Picture this scenario: you go to register for an event. Rather than just writing your name on a stick-on name tag, you have to go to a website or an app and fill out all your contact details. You then stand in line and get, what, wait for it, your name printed on a name tag. Wow, that was so worth it.

Here is another example. Your business is transitioning to a new CRM system. You have about 10,000 customers in your existing database. It seems to be an automatic given that all the customer data must be transferred from the old system, regardless of the quality of the information in that customer data or the regularity of business provided by each of those customers.

This transfer process typically involves a large number of long team meetings, an outside database consultant, and an expensive data portability process. In most cases, having the data entered from scratch into the new system is a far better solution. Properly trained data entry staff will help trap duplicate account names, contact details, product number inaccuracies, and all manner of data corruption issues. This work would also be done by non-project-critical staff and at a far lower cost.

By using the "sledgehammer" of human entry you would end up with a cleaner database for far less money, and get it done on a parallel project path. Sounds like a winner to me.

The Common Sense Approach here is to choose the right tool for the task even if that tool comes out of the old-school toolbox.

Sloth

So many people today are working, in one form or another, just about 24/7. Smart phones, communication apps, and the never-ending news cycle have really fractured our attention. People multi-task, Skype, email, Twitter, what-have-you, in a mad rush to be first.

All of this has led people to work more and more. That much is certain. However, I'm not sure all this work has led to more productivity or more efficiency. This is why I am motivated by sloth.

Yes, you read that right: I am motivated by sloth. I am not talking about being idle, for sloths are not idle. I am talking about expending the appropriate amount of effort necessary to obtain what is needed. I prefer to work very hard right up until I get things functioning just right and then it seems that I'm not working at all.

My goal, and the goal I try to inspire in others, is to reach a place where one can get the optimal amount of work done with the minimal amount of effort.

Contrary to general understanding, the sloth can actually move with great speed when required. If speed is not required, then the sloth moves slowly. Basically, the sloth always moves at the appropriate speed for the situation at hand.

Under normal circumstances, the sloth moves very slowly, and only when necessary. Sloths have strong bodies which, over time, have actually changed their metabolism to operate at the optimal pace.

When providing consulting services, I often have to slow the client down for their own benefit. The instinct is to move fast. However, this instinct often does more harm than good.

Most businesses do not operate at the optimal pace. Most businesses rush and whirl from project to project, from sale to sale, from new trend to new trend.

Now, I am not objecting to businesses moving fast. Neither am I advocating for businesses to move too slowly. I'm suggesting that each business should find the optimal level of speed to best ensure its survival.

More often than not, maximum speed leads to inefficiencies, inconsistencies, or worse.

The Common Sense Approach here is to expend only the appropriate level of energy and move at the appropriate pace. Work as hard as you must to put things in place so that it doesn't seem like you are working hard at all. It would be a sin to not get this right.

Smart Money

Many business people have told me that their firms are looking for investment. Some seek start-up funding, some an angel round, or even V.C. funding. You may be looking to bring an idea to market, accelerate your development timetable, or expand into a new factory or a new warehouse. Whatever business stage you are in and whatever you intend to do with this influx of capital, the reality is your company needs money.

The first step here is to ensure that you **need** the money and not just that you **want** the money. This is the first step, since whatever your answer is will determine the rest of your journey. Now, I'm very happy to come and help you with the decision process for this step. However, that usually takes three or four days, much more time than we have available here.

So, let's move forward with the assumption that you do actually need the money. Now you need to understand the difference between Smart Money and Dumb Money. The terms Smart Money and Dumb Money refer only to the money itself and not the intelligence of the people behind the money.

Smart Money comes with plenty of additional aspects. Smart Money comes with things like significant experience in markets like yours, strong connections with key target customers and distribution partners, and positive relationships with media outlets that help shape the opinions of influential thinkers who are important to your business.

Smart Money may even come with direct connections and business deals with related firms that can help you grow much faster than just the money could. You see, Smart Money, and those who give it to you, are very deeply aligned with your success. They will invest their time, their skills, their connections, and other non-monetary things into your business.

By contrast, Dumb Money comes with little more than a terms sheet and a payment plan. These are financial investments made with the core idea of getting a return on the investment. It is important to state that the people behind Dumb Money can still be very smart. However, they are looking at the numbers, the projections, and pay-outs that you will, hopefully, provide to them. Dumb Money basically stops any meaningful involvement once the check is cut. Dumb Money people just don't, can't, or won't include any investment in your company beyond the money itself. They absolutely want you to be successful, and to share in that success. They just feel that their part of the partnership is to provide funding and not much more.

If you have determined that capital is all that is required, then Dumb Money may be a great fit for your needs. If your firm is hitting on most cylinders and all you need is a cash boost to complete a product cycle, fund a marketing campaign, or bring on some much needed extra staff, Dumb Money might be perfect. They bring the money, you deploy it as you see fit, and everybody gets what they want and need.

Once you determine that you *need* the money, you need to include the type of money you will get as you decide which funders you are willing to accept into your business family. Because of the non-monetary benefits of Smart Money, you may well be able to get by with a smaller investment that you originally estimated. And, because of the money-first focus of Dumb Money, you may need more money than you first thought.

As all this is happening, remember that the company is yours and **you** get to choose who gets to be part of it. The transaction is, in essence, a partnership. You are bringing your company, your products, your ideas, and your energy. The investors, depending on the type, are bringing money or perhaps a lot more than that.

The Common Sense Approach here is to realize that there are different types of money and they have different uses. As you review your pool of potential investors, be sure you remember that some Smart Money may be better than a lot of Dumb Money.

Taxi

It would seem that Uber and Lyft have gone from being just ideas to market disrupters to business labels in a few short years. By "business label" I mean that other firms include them in their pitches, saying that they are, or want to be, the Uber-Of-This-Market or the Lyft-Of-That-Market.

While these business stories are well known, today I would like you to consider two aspects that aren't regularly covered.

First, a great deal of fuss is made about Uber's amazing technology. It's interesting, perhaps; but amazing? No. Uber has stitched together a series of other people's tech (maps, GPS, e-payments, etc.) to do a job that has been done for decades via radio dispatchers and by a taxi driver's knowledge of the area. A good use of technology? Certainly. Amazing? Not really.

Second, Uber's success is mainly attributed to their amazing business idea. Again I say; interesting, perhaps, but amazing, no. Uber, and similar services like Lyft, were **initially** successful because of their business idea. Their **continued** success is dependent on the apathy and ineptitude of their legacy competitors, the taxi companies.

On the technology front, Uber and Lyft may be able to stay ahead of the other ride share services. They may also get "jumped" by some other firm that does them one better on the tech front. As an example, all a company would need to do is link your next ride directly into your calendar. Those companies already know when and where your meetings take place, when your flights leave, or when your child's football game starts. They could then offer this service directly, or license it to the taxi firms.

On the business front, if the taxi companies ever wake up and understand what is actually happening, they might just adjust their business models and recapture a great deal of the riders. Uber isn't primarily solving a driver/rider problem. I still need to get in a car and have the driver take me someplace. The drive takes as long as it takes. In fact, in a taxi the ride is generally faster. Rather, Uber and Lyft solve the frustration of taxi rides being hard to get. It is often too much work to get a cab where and when you want one. If a rider could summon a taxi as easily, the need for an Uber or Lyft type of service would drop dramatically.

The Common Sense Approach here is to understand the shiny new business thing and to understand the **why** behind the disruption. Then, adjust your business accordingly to either stop or expand on the w**hy**.

Now, I gotta go; my ride is here.

The Joy of UX

I'm just going to come out and say it...The greatest user experience on the entire internet is the Google search box. There, I said it.

The search box is perfect. It has just one feature... Search. The user knows exactly what to do and the system does exactly what the user wants.

Rather than make the user guess, Search only lets you do one thing.

No extra clutter. No mind-numbing string of videos, radio buttons, or anything else the user doesn't need. Google Search is the exact UX that everybody wants.

So many sites are over-designed, over-engineered, and over-complicated. Marketing wants the user to bend this way. Sales wants the user to bend that way. Customer Service has these needs. All of this leads to frustration *of* rather than service *to* the user. UX should never be about what you want. It should be only about what the user wants.

Many of my consulting clients come to me for help integrating technology into their business. Interestingly, many of them are technology companies. You see, just because smart people know *how* to build great software doesn't necessary mean they are smart about *what* to build.

UX should be an intimate thing. Keeping the desires of the user as the center of your efforts is a great way to start building a great UX.

Now, I love designers and I respect the critical role they play in making the web work. I'm just frustrated with the lack of balance between what the company wants and what the user wants.

Don't tease your user with the promise of an exciting experience and then lead them down an unsatisfying series of clicks and buttons.

Don't fake it with the user by presenting them with interesting style sheets and designs, only to leave them dissatisfied with the experience.

So many firms want to put every conceivable feature or function into every screen. This leads to busy and cluttered software and so many options that it turns off, rather than excites, the user.

The Common Sense Approach here is to be 100% focused on the needs of the user as you do your design. Your goal should be to please them. If they are happy then you should be, too. After all, isn't that what UX is all about?

The Nature of Business

Too many businesses today are focused on things like technology and just-in-time inventory management, all by way of pushing everything harder and faster. We are always seeking to do things at super speeds, and are even releasing products that are just barely ready. In fact, we have lost sight of the natural way of doing things. By natural way, I mean the natural flow of business and the way that nature does things.

As most of the country's work began to shift from growing crops and raising livestock to manufacturing and distributing products, most businesses followed the same natural paths and timing that controlled life on the farm. Work hours even used to reflect the same dawn-to-dusk schedule.

Through the decades, we have incorporated a great deal of nature's words into our business lingo, but we have lost most of nature's pacing and patience. You would be hard-pressed to read a business plan or marketing strategy without encountering any number of words or phrases from the natural world.

We have buying and selling **seasons**

We **prune** expenses

We provide **seed funding** for new businesses and then we **incubate** them

We set aside budget dollars in **rainy-day** funds

We manufacture in **plants**

We put our servers in **farms**

And so on and so on. Conversely, you would be even more hard-pressed to find many businesses that understand and respect the way nature orders and organizes things. When was the last time you heard of a business allowing itself to hibernate until conditions improved?

What was the last company you remember that was happy to let some profits go unrealized so that its production line could lay fallow and its workers take a rest and recover?

Have you ever heard of a business not expending all of its resources to gather all the nectar of profits this year even though it may well have a negative impact on next year?

Just because the speed of business has quickened, we should not abandon the natural process of business. We still need to exercise discipline in product development, manufacturing, and customer service, even though these processes are constantly being updated via the use of technology.

The Common Sense Approach here is for your business to consider its customers, suppliers, workers, and shareholders as natural resources that need to be tended, nurtured, and sustained for the long haul. After all, winter is coming.

The Old Country

Everybody in America is getting older. Many people view this as bad news. I disagree 100%. Aging presents all sorts of opportunities. Opportunities for the people aging and for those who wish to serve them.

Advertisers and marketers are obsessed with the 18-34 demographic. This never really made any sense. That coveted age group has low incomes and high expenses. It's largely made up of high school and college students, recent college grads with their student loans, and young parents, most of whom have almost no financial strength or flexibility.

Yes, this younger group can be more easily swayed to spend on trendy items. However, trendy is constantly changing and expensive for firms to get right. This creates a vicious cycle of company spending in order to chase the whims of a trendy audience.

Now let's look at the older crowd. In the 2010 census there were over 40 million Americans aged 65 or older. To provide some context, by itself that group would constitute the 33rd largest country in the world. That is a lot of customers.

This isn't a one-time thing. The projected numbers for the 2020 census show that there will be about 55 million U.S. citizens in the 65+ category. The population over 60 is actually growing faster than the population under 45.

Does your business plan take these figures into account? Are you building new products and services for this market segment? This group has solid income, very low debt, and lots of free time. Are you ready to serve them?

Other than pharmaceutical firms, it seems that nobody is paying any attention to this market. Why is that? Well, this group doesn't always look pretty in glossy ads, and they can't be as easily fooled as the younger shoppers. But, in reality, the 65+ group consistently has more buying power than the younger one.

At my consulting firm we spend a lot of time exploring target markets for our clients' products and services. When shown the hard demographic data, the client is often willing to do the self-examination necessary and to see how they can sell to these markets.

It might not be sexy to sell to older folks. However, it is profitable. They are willing to pay for quality products. They have high loyalty tendencies and they are good at actual word-of-mouth marketing.

These people have money. They are not fickle consumers. They appreciate both high quality products and good service. Should you be ignoring them?

The Common Sense Approach here is to get the hard data on potential markets and then make the hard decisions to adjust your firm to address the largest possible pool of customers. Do that, and your firm will be one for the ages.

Three-Legged Stool

This chapter is a variance of a story told to me by my friend Steve. It's about the three-legged stool concept of running a business. Thanks for getting me started on this one, Steve.

The core idea of the story is that in order to properly stand, all legs of the three-legged stool must be intact. Any leg being too short, too long, or too weak, and the whole company falls down.

Many have told this story in some form or another and many more will continue to tell it. Steve's form had the three legs representing *customers*, *employees*, and *shareholders*. This is the best three-legged balance I have ever heard.

Various tellers of the tale will switch out one leg for another, perhaps using *innovation* or *products* as one of the legs, perhaps using *community* or *marketplace*.

Regardless of how one labels the three legs of the stool, to me the critical issue is the delicate balance between the three legs. You see, there are plenty of three-legged stools that don't stand properly. Just having three legs doesn't take you all the way to success.

The most important thing in the story, and by extension in your business, is the precious balance between the three. I like Steve's choices, so I'll stick with customers, employees, and shareholders.

I often work with my consulting clients helping them establish and then keep this delicate balance in place. Sometimes it requires an outside view to see the problem properly. Since I can look at the stool from a distance, it is easier for me to see points of imbalance that may not be apparent internally.

Do your overriding business principles strive to keep the needs and wants of your customers, employees, and shareholders in balance? Do your shareholders feel employee pay is having a negative impact on dividends? Do your policies demonstrate that you love your customers more than your employees? By definition, no leg of your stool can be more important or more deserving than the others.

Balance, as always, is a tricky thing indeed. Even keeping two forces in balance can be very taxing. Establishing and keeping a three-way balance takes tremendous focus and constant vigilance.

It is hard work. It is easy-peasy, however, compared to the much harder work of trying to keep a company that is out of balance functioning properly.

The Common Sense Approach here is to drive all of your decisions with the full understanding of the impact they will have on the overall balance of the three-legged stool. If the balance is off, the whole stool—and your company with it—will break apart and topple to the ground.

Traffic Lights

Portland, Maine, and Portland, Oregon, are just under 3,200 miles apart by the most efficient direct road route. That route would take you through about 15 states and require almost 48 hours of driving time, most likely spread over several days of calendar time.

That information, combined with the most basic knowledge of U.S. geography, should be enough detail to enable any rational and motivated person to make a decent enough outline and then get started moving east to west on their journey.

I used the qualifiers "should" and "most" to highlight the fact that there are people out there—who knows how many—who would not even think of getting started on such a journey without a great deal more detail.

Planning is an important part of any scheduled venture. You will get no argument from me on that. The argument will be based on how much planning is enough. Especially enough to get started.

Using the Portland to Portland trip as an example, there are people out there who would like to know the color of every traffic light between the two cities before they would head out into the New England morning. This information is, of course, both unknowable and un-important.

Unknowable because by the time all that data are gathered and absorbed by the driver, they will have changed. Unimportant because the color of all the traffic lights beyond the next two or three would most likely have no meaningful impact on the overall journey.

Holding progress hostage waiting for this level of detail is unhelpful to your business and unhealthy for your mind.

Some of the clients I work with in my consulting practice bring me in specifically to address the knowledge requirement conflicts that arise within their businesses.

The struggle over how much information is required to move forward is a crippler of innovation and a tremendous waste of resources. The speed of business today, especially the speed of your competitors, is simply too rapid to allow for a complete review of all the facts you may wish to see.

If you can drive a car, know east from west, can read maps and street signs or even use a GPS, how much additional data do you really need to get started on a journey like this?

At what point will you stop delaying and start working towards the goal of reaching your destination?

The Common Sense Approach here is to know where you are, where you want to go, and which direction will take you there. Get moving, gather new data as the road before you unfolds. Most of all, get your head out of the reports and enjoy the ride.

Worry

If you listen to business pundits today, you will hear a long list of things about which you should worry. They will tell you to worry about cyber security, about foreign exchange rates, about Chinese imports, about market pressures, and about dropping share prices. These are some of the same people who ask questions like, "What keeps you up at night?"

Well, I'm here to tell you not to worry about any of those things. In fact, I'm here to tell you not to worry about anything at all. There, I hope you feel better.

Now, before you get too comfortable, you need to understand *why* I'm telling you not to worry. Well, it isn't because all those problems mentioned above, and plenty of others, don't exist, and that they aren't threats to your business.

No, the reason I'm telling you not to worry is because worrying is a complete waste of resources. A waste of time, of money, and of intellect. You will gain nothing from worrying. In fact, if you worry about these things you will only make everything worse.

Nobody sets out to worry. Nobody calls a Worry Meeting. However, worry does tend to creep into our thinking.

This entire topic often surfaces in both my consulting practice and in my public speaking work. People tend to not react well when I run off a list of potential threats and then tell them it is not a good idea to worry about them.

That is fair enough.

My consulting clients and I spend a fair amount of time setting aside worry and turning our minds towards solutions. The truth of the matter is that you do need to be *aware* of these threats. You do need to understand their causes and their potential impacts on your business. However, you should *not* worry about them.

Rather than worrying about the problems your business is facing, *do something*. What you should do is dissect the problems, build action plans to address them, and then set about reducing, if not eliminating them.

I urge you to take positive actions like the ones I mentioned rather than getting caught up in and paralyzed by worry. No problem was every solved by worrying. No corrective action was ever taken by worrying.

Worry will cripple your thinking, your creativity, and possibly your whole company. In my entire life, personal and professional, I have never encountered a single circumstance when worry helped anybody do anything.

The Common Sense Approach here is to recognize the problems your business is facing, meet them head on, and then *do* something about them. If you do that, day in and day out, you will have nothing *to worry about*.

Yeah, But...

In one of my books, *Kill The First Tiger*, there are stories about tigers, zombies, and other dangerous beasts out there in the workplace jungle. While each of those is a real threat to your business, there are two other sinister creatures lurking about. These creatures are even more dangerous because they blend in so well and seem so innocuous.

I'm referring here to possibly the two most destructive internal forces in business today; the YEAHBUT and the JUSTA. These two will suck the creativity, innovation, and motivation right out of your business without you even noticing their presence.

Many of you have seen the YEAHBUT in action. That person who after each innovative solution, product idea, or process improvement suggestion says, "Yeah, but..." and then continues in mock support of the idea while destroying every aspect of it. First saying "YEAH" and then after that killer comma it follows with the "BUT." This creates the illusion that they agree and then shows the truth that they do not. This is a toxic fume that kills the spirit of the problem solvers. This is a dangerous beast, indeed. However, at least the YEAHBUT reveals itself to those who are paying attention.

No matter how dangerous the YEAHBUT is to your firm, the JUSTA is an even larger threat. You see, the JUSTA is lurking almost everywhere yet is very rarely seen. The call of the JUSTA is regularly heard, but rarely identified. You ask the opinion of the person in the lobby and they say, "I'm JUSTA receptionist, how would I know?" You ask the warehouse foreman about shipping policies and you get, "I'm JUSTA guy who works for a living." Sadly, many employees at most firms are some kind of JUSTA.

While I'm consulting with a business, I always seek to find these creatures and tell the client about them. The YEAHBUT will drain valuable time and creative thinking from your business, while the JUSTA hides significant potential across your business.

The YEAHBUT and the JUSTA exist in almost every business. One crushes good ideas and discussions and the other prevents innovation from ever even surfacing. Most organizations do not get as much out of their employees as they should. If the YEAHBUT and the JUSTA are allowed to roam free, the employees contribute even less. Are you letting these creatures roam the halls of your business?

The Common Sense Approach here is to listen carefully to what all your employees are saying and to be on constant lookout for the YEAHBUT and the JUSTA. It is very possible that some good ideas are being trashed by the YEAHBUT and that the JUSTA is stopping other good ideas from ever coming out. It is your role to find and stop these creatures before they cripple your business.

Your Call

All you have to do is pay a little bit of attention to advertisements, press releases, and other public statements from businesses to realize that there are a few standard phrases in use today that nobody truly believes but people seem to accept nevertheless.

Perhaps the best–or maybe the worst–example is that of the outright lie that various recorded voices tell millions of callers every day. Yes, I'm talking about the dreaded, "Your Call Is Important To Us," line that is on almost every automated call system in America.

Let's think about this for a minute. If our call was truly important, wouldn't the business we were calling have a person available to take it? If you and I were having a meeting and I said, "Your thoughts are important to me," and then I held up my hand to stop you from talking, how would you react? If you and I were having dinner and I said, "I really want to hear what you have to say," and then I excused myself and left you at the table, would you believe that I really wanted to hear what you had to say?

Why is it, then, that so many businesses get to tell the "Your call is important" lie to us millions of times a day? Why does your business do it? Why do you allow yourself to be lied to when you call one of these numbers?

My view is that most businesses see customer service as an expense rather than as a relationship-building opportunity. Tricked by the calculations of the automated phone vendors and misled by the internal presentations of the VP of Customer Satisfaction, or some such title, businesses have convinced themselves that telling this particular lie is somehow *better* for the business and its customers than just actually answering the phone call.

Customer satisfaction and loyalty can be both a key differentiator and a key profitability driver. Keep in mind it is the customer–*not* the phone software firm–that buys things from you and allows you to stay in business. Customers are calling because they have a problem. Why don't you want to help them?

A lot of the consulting work I do is around helping corporations effectively and efficiently deploy technology to enhance the customer's overall experience. Rest assured, not answering phone calls is not one of my suggested paths to customer happiness.

A stunning exception to this anti-customer approach is L.L. Bean. Honest to God, I just stopped working on this chapter and called them. Two rings later I was talking to a live person who I truly felt wanted to help me. Bean is a $1.5 billion company that processes tons of orders for tons of customers every day, mostly clothes and outdoor wear. There is virtually no technology in their products. Yet they invest the resources to have actual people answer the phone.

I tried the same experiment with both Microsoft and Apple. In each case, I got an automated version of the "Important" lie. These are much larger companies than Bean, with billions of dollars sitting idle in their corporate accounts. They are businesses based almost entirely on technology, yet they don't want to actually talk to me if they can avoid it.

How or why does Bean answer calls with actual people? There is no magical answer, no super secret. It is simply a matter of leadership and priorities. The reality is that to L.L. Bean my call was really, actually, important to them. Even after I explained I was just working on an essay, the customer rep. asked me if there was anything she could do to help.

When you are done with this chapter, call your company's customer service number and see what happens. In fact, go ahead and send me the number and I'll call myself.

The Common Sense Approach here is for businesses to be constantly looking for ways to be efficient and effective so the customers don't have to call in the first place, but, when they do call, consider having a real person pick up the phone and actually help them.

About the Author

Michael Johnson has over 30 years' worth of hard-fought and hard-taught business experience, from his early days in retail, through his computer design and programming work, and into his role as a corporate strategy expert.

Michael's experience runs the gamut from being the founder of a start-up that folded before it could make its first sale, through a variety of small business and corporate positions, all the way to a buyer and seller of several companies.

His work has taken him to 15 countries spanning five continents.

Born and raised in the Washington, D.C area, Michael now lives with his lovely bride (of 25+ years) in the woods of Southeastern Wisconsin.

Michael is a regular speaker at a variety of events and conferences. In addition to his writing and speaking work, Michael runs a strategic consulting firm called Full Potential Associates.

More information about Michael can be found at his corporate website: http://fullpotentialassociates.com/

And at his public speaker website: http://www.mfjspeaker.com/

Reach Michael directly: mfj@mfjspeaker.com

To arrange to have Michael speak at your next event, email: info@mfjspeaker.com